M561 Gama Goat

Written by David Doyle

Detail In Action®

Squadron Signal Publications

Cover Art by Don Greer

(Front Cover) Thanks to its flexible, two-unit body, the Gama Goat boasted remarkable off-road capabilities. The vehicle's complicated drive train, however, made for labor-intensive maintenance. This drawback, combined with rising weight and costs, and notable engine noise, served to limit procurement of the vehicle.

(Back Cover) Serving at home and deployed to Europe and Korea, the Gama Goat was used by both the U.S. Army and the Marine Corps. The vehicle's only combat experience, however, took place in Grenada in 1983.

About the Detail In Action® Series

Detail In Action books trace the development of a single type of aircraft, armored vehicle, or ship from prototype to use. The equipment is shown in action and then specific close-up details of important sections of the equipment are explained. Experimental or "one-off" variants can also be included. Our first *In Action®* book was printed in 1971.

Squadron/Signal Walk Around® books feature the best surviving and restored historic aircraft and vehicles. Inevitably, the requirements of preservation, restoration, exhibit, and continued use may affect these examples in some details of paint and equipment. Authors strive to highlight any feature that departs from original specifications.

Hardcover ISBN 978-0-89747-735-2
Softcover ISBN 978-0-89747-736-9

Proudly printed in the U.S.A.
Copyright 2013 Squadron/Signal Publications
1115 Crowley Drive, Carrollton, TX 75006-1312 U.S.A.
www.SquadronSignalPublications.com

All rights reserved. No part of this publication may be reproduced, stored in a retrieval system, or transmitted in any form by means electrical, mechanical, or otherwise, without written permission of the publisher.

Military/Combat Photographs and Snapshots

If you have any photos of aircraft, armor, soldiers, or ships of any nation, particularly wartime snapshots, please share them with us and help make Squadron/Signal's books all the more interesting and complete in the future. Any photograph sent to us will be copied and returned. Electronic images are preferred. The donor will be fully credited for any photos used. Please send them to the address above.

(Title Page) The highly flexible Gama Goat stands as one of the U.S. military's most unique wheeled vehicles.

Acknowledgments

As always, creating this book required a great deal of help from a number of people. On this project, I was blessed to have the help of Bill Janowski, a member of the original Gama Goat design team. Also key to bringing this book about were Tom Kailbourn, John Adams-Graf, the late Fred Crismon, Kevin Emdee, Luther Hanson, Randy Talbot, Pat Ware, Jeff Rowsam, Scott Taylor, as well as the staff of the Military Vehicle Preservation Association's publication Army Motors. Thanks also to Don Meinhardt for allowing me to photograph his superbly restored M561. As always, many of the archival photos on these pages were scanned by my long-suffering wife Denise, and the great team at Squadron Publications went the extra mile to make the photos and the words look – and read – at their best.

Introduction

The United States military has through the years tended to strive to equip itself with vehicles capable of going anywhere. From the earliest motor transport convoys across the west, engineers of military vehicles have wrestled with a major shortcoming of conventional vehicles – namely, the rigid chassis. The rigid chassis limits the amount of flex that a vehicle can have, and absent extremely long suspension travel, the result is one or more wheels lifting from the ground. When a wheel is not contacting the ground, not only is not supplying traction, but it is also not available to carry a share of the load.

Naturally, these problems were not unique to the United States, nor the military. In the late 1950s the Swiss army began seeking a new vehicle. In response Swiss tractor manufacturer Ernst Meili developed a 6x6 vehicle with hydraulic pitch control system, a system for which he filed a patent in 1957.

Meili's vehicle, dubbed the Metrac, used hydraulic cylinders to provide positive pitch control. This control allowed the vehicle to climb vertical walls nearly three feet tall. While an interesting and capable vehicle, it was handicapped by being expensive and somewhat ungainly to operate. Meili licensed his patent to others, who attempted to market the unusual vehicles at the 1960 Geneva Motor show, to no avail.

The vehicle did come to the attention of the US military. Clark Equipment Company, of Battle Creek, Michigan, was licensed to produce vehicles using Meili's patents, and produced two prototype vehicles for testing by the army and Marines.

An advantage of a six-wheeled vehicle with a hydraulically operated suspension was the ability to flex the vehicle in order to surmount steep obstacles such as might be found in forward areas. The Clark Flex-Trac demonstrates that ability on a tall block of concrete. (USMC)

The Flex-Trac has mounted the concrete block and is balanced on its center wheels. The snub nose of the forward section, or tractor, and the slanted rear face of the rear section, the carrier, were designed to allow the tires to engage obstructions. (USMC)

The front end of the tractor section of the Flex-Trac has landed on the ground and the rest of the vehicle soon will follow. Chains were fitted on the 7.50-20 tires for added traction. Power was provided by a Willys F-head four-cylinder engine rated at 72 horsepower. (USMC)

In an effort to field a high-mobility cargo carrier capable of operating in rough terrain in forward areas, in the early 1960s the U.S. Army became interested in the Swiss-manufactured Meili Metrac, a six-wheeled vehicle with hinged joints between the forward and rear sections. The Metrac also featured a sophisticated hydraulic suspension that allowed the front "tractor" component to flex and enabled the vehicle to level itself laterally when operating on slopes. Aberdeen Proving Ground acquired and tested a Metrac in 1961, and Clark Equipment Company of Battle Creek, Michigan, secured the rights to produce a version of the Metrac, dubbed the Flex-Trac, seen here during testing in the mid-1960s. (Fred Crismon Collection)

The center wheels of the Clark Flex-Trac are about to land on the ground, while the rear wheels are still poised atop the concrete block, ready to descend. The angled rear of the carrier, which enhanced the angle of departure, is particularly evident from this angle. (USMC)

Like the Meili Metrac, the Clark Flex-Trac had a sophisticated hydraulic system for lowering selected wheels in order to drive down slopes while the vehicle remained laterally level. This Flex-Trac is negotiating a slope without adjusting the wheel height. (USMC)

A Clark Flex-Trac demonstrates its ability to drive through thick mud. A close examination of the photo reveals that chains are installed on the tires. Although intended principally for operation on land, the Flex-Trac also had an amphibious capability. (USMC)

A Clark Flex-Trac enters a river during a test or demonstration of its amphibious abilities. This example has a water propeller on what appears to be a hydraulically extended shaft on each side of the tractor. This feature is clearer in a subsequent photo. (USMC)

With a driver wearing a life jacket at the controls, the Clark Flex-Trac chugs across a river. The bodies of the tractor and the carrier components were designed to be watertight. Steering of the vehicle while navigating in water was by the front wheels. (USMC)

The Clark Flex-Trac had an overall length of about 144 inches, a width of 82 inches, and a height of 74 inches. At first glance it appeared to be a small tractor towing a carrier, but the two main body components were intended to operate together as a system. (Fred Crismon collection)

As the Flex-Trac emerges from the river, the water-propeller shaft and what appear to be a brace and/or actuating strut are visible on the left side. The logo of the Clark Equipment Company was marked on several places on the tractor and carrier components. (USMC)

In this 1960s demonstration, a Clark Flex-Trac surmounts an obstacle with a ditch in front. A man in a white lab coat drives while in the background, military personnel and civilians seated on bleachers watch the proceedings. (Fred Crismon collection)

A Flex-Trac demonstrates its climbing abilities on a wooden obstacle in the mid-1960s. The cylinder and rod stretching from the rear of the tractor component to behind the wheel on the carrier component was part of the pitch control mechanism. (Fred Crismon collection)

A driver, possibly the same one in the preceding photo, carefully drives a Flex-Trac down a wall on a test course. On the top center of the rear of the body of the carrier component was a prominent cutout. The upper edges of the carrier body were rolled. (Fred Crismon collection)

During the winter, a Flex-Trac negotiates an icy slough on a test course. The success of the tests of the Flex-Trac led the U.S. military to pursue, with Chance Vought Corp., the concept of a similar 6x6 cargo vehicle, but without the complicated hydraulics. (Fred Crismon collection)

Gama Goat

Half a world away in Fawnskin, California, was inventor and tool maker Roger Gamaunt. In March 1947, predating Ernst Meili's efforts by a decade, Gamaunt was laying out the design of a six-wheel, two-body vehicle. Gamaunt, a prolific inventor and vehicle consultant, moved on to other projects. However, in 1959 Chance Vought Aircraft Incorporated sought to diversify from military aviation. Among the markets they looked into were ground vehicles.

By July of that year contact had been made between Gamount and Vought, and by October of that year a contract had been executed between the parties. This contract called for Gamaunt to produce, within 10 months, a working prototype of his six-wheel vehicle. The contract also stipulated that title of the prototype was to transfer to Gamaunt after testing was completed.

A licensing agreement was also entered into that required Chance Vought to apply for a patent on the Gama Goat at Vought's expense and in Gamaunt's name. Such paperwork was filed on 13 April, 1960, and in May 1965 patent number 183991 was issued for same.

Fabrication of the prototype began in Gamaunt's Fawnskin shop, but by July 1960, despite Vought having fabricated the bodies and shipped them to California, the decision had been made to transfer the project to the Chance Vought plant in Grand Prarie, Texas. This was done in an effort to expedite production.

To power the unique aluminum vehicle and maintain a low weight, an air-cooled Corvair automobile engine was selected as the power plant. Testing of the vehicle by Chance Vought began on 4 October 1960 – however problems with the steering system delayed these efforts for some time.

By early 1961 the performance was such that the company, by then having lost the "Aircraft" from its name, was ready to demonstrate the Gama Goat to the Army. Gamaunt, along with engineer William Janowski, showed the machine's abilities at the Ordnance Tank-Automotive Command; the Artillery Board at Fort Sill; the Infantry School at Fort Benning, and the Armor Board at Fort Knox, as well as the Marines at Quantico. With the observers suitably impressed, in March 1961 Chance Vought submitted a proposal for the vehicle to the military. This proposal was rejected, as the Ordnance Tank-Automotive Command was intent on soliciting proposals in August for a new 1 ¼-ton vehicle. It was felt Chance Vought should wait for this solicitation.

Roger Gamaunt, designer and manufacturer of the prototype Gama Goat, shows off the vehicle to two executive secretaries of Chance Vought. An engineering designer and consultant, he had begun preliminary design work on a six-wheeled, rough-terrain, two-body cargo vehicle in 1947. In October 1959, Chance Vought contracted with Gamaunt to manufacture such a prototype vehicle, which would be known as the Gama Goat. (Bill Janowski collection)

The prototype Gama Goat was rolled out on 30 September 1960, and the following month it completed its initial test program, including assessments of its mobility, swimming and flotation, and airlift capabilities. In one such test, the vehicle emerges from a cargo aircraft with a full complement of eight troops in the carrier component, along with the driver and a passenger in the tractor component. On the tractor was the Chance Vought logo. (Bill Janowski collection)

The prototype Gama Goat undergoes cross-country mobility testing near the Chance Vought plant in Grand Paririe, Texas. Texas license plate 2Y-7999 is affixed to the front of the body. At the wheel was William R. Janowski, a member of the design team. (Bill Janowski collection)

Soldiers take the prototype Gama Goat for a test drive. By now, the vehicle had been engaged in tests and demonstrations at a number of military bases. The stickers below the "GAMA GOAT" inscription on the carrier represent those military installations. (TACOM LCMC History Office)

During the early days of the VTOL (vertical takeoff and landing) cargo-aircraft program, the Gama Goat prototype is on the ramp of a VTOL fuselage mockup. Mounted on the front of the body is a spare tire and, to its left, a civilian license plate. Originally this vehicle had no spare, but the military insisted upon the inclusion of one at this stage – a decision which was reversed on the production vehicles. (Kevin Emdee Collection)

Rough, hilly terrain provides an ideal test course for the prototype Gama Goat with a full cargo of troops in a Detroit Arsenal photograph dated 21 August 1962. The flexible, two-body-component design of the Gama Goat allowed it to flex and conform to the terrain in ways that a conventional cargo vehicle would never be able to. On the front of the tractor is the 27-7999 Texas license plate. (TACOM LCMC History Office)

A driver takes the prototype Gama Goat through its paces during Transportation Corps demonstrations at Fort Eustis, Virginia. On the right side of the front deck is a fire extinguisher. Bucket seats were provided in the tractor cab for the driver and a passenger. Braces were on the sides of the windshield, and a single brace was at the front center of the windshield. To the rear of the tractor cab was the cover for the engine compartment. (Kevin Emdee Collection)

The center of the Gama Goat prototype flexes downward as the vehicle crosses a gully at Fort Eustis. Inside the carrier component, framing is visible in the form of vertical members fastened with gussets to a horizontal member along the top of the body.

During the demonstration for the Transportation Corps at Fort Eustis, the prototype Gama Goat shows its ability to swim. Two mufflers and exhausts were installed on the upper rear corners of the tractor body; the left ones are visible here, with the tailpipe turned up. (Kevin Emdee Collection)

The Gama Goat prototype takes part in a demonstration at Fort Eustis, Virginia. There is a semicircular tunnel at the bottom center of the carrier's rear. Below the left reflector and tail light is Texas 1960 truck license plate 2X-4886. (Kevin Emdee Collection)

Now mounted with a front winch and bearing U.S. Army markings, the prototype Gama Goat tackles a rough course during a U.S. Army air-mobility symposium at Fort Benning, Georgia, in August 1963. The carrier is fitted with a waterproof cover. (US Army Quartermaster Museum)

LTV Gama Goat

During the fall of 1961 Gamaunt's Gama Goat had been demonstrated at various military installations in the continental U.S. as well as in Germany and France. Over 6,000 miles, relatively trouble-free, had been put on the vehicle. Thus, when in December 1961 the Military Characteristics of a replacement for the Dodge M37 ¾-ton 4x4 truck were published, the Gama Goat was ready. The characteristics, entitled "Truck, Utility, High Mobility, Light Duty, XM561," defined the vehicle which the June 1961 Development Project OCTM 37758 had initiated.

In July, Chance Vought became a division of Ling-Temco-Vought (LTV) and the Army began soliciting bids for design of prototype vehicles adhering to its Military Characteristics. Meanwhile Gamaunt's prototype continued to put on various demonstrations around the world, including several months of operation in Thailand under the auspices of the Advanced Research Project Agency. These operations, with Bill Janowski at the wheel, were the subject of the Vought marketing film *The Goat in Thailand*.

In March of 1963 LTV was awarded a contract to fabricate two Test Rig XM561 vehicles and fourteen prototype vehicles. Nine of these were to be powered by a special version of the General Motors (GM), Detroit Diesel Division 3-53 Diesel engine featuring an aluminum block, while the remaining five would be powered by an experimental Lycoming air-cooled multi-fuel engine.

Test Rig was defined by Army Material Command and Automotive-Tank-Armament Command as being a full-scale operable vehicle built under expedited conditions generally representing the military prototype. It was understood that one of the test rigs would be retained by LTV while the other was supplied to the military for testing.

The first of these vehicles, Army registration number 3E3108, was rolled out in December 1963, while the second vehicle, registration number 3E3109, was completed in February 1964. This vehicle was delivered to Aberdeen Proving Ground. These vehicles and the 14 prototypes looked markedly different both from Gamaunt's initial vehicle and from the later mass-produced vehicles. The body styling was different, and the vehicles had conventional brake drums vs. the sealed external drums used in production.

The change from conventional brake drums to sealed external brake drums followed testing of the second pilot at Aberdeen. It was found during the military testing that mud could migrate into the brake drums, as well as steering and universal joints, leading to premature wear. This in turn led to intensive maintenance, and numerous alterations in the design were made to combat this.

Also as a result of the Aberdeen tests, the spare tire, upon which the military had previously insisted, was replaced by a 'get home' truss kit. The intent of the truss kit was that in the event of a flat, the flat tire would be moved to a center position (and the displaced good tire moved to the former position of the flat. The installed truss kit would lock out the body flexibility, making the Gama Goat rigid and allow it to operate on five wheels.

Further improvements stemming from the Aberdeen tests were the addition of bilge pumps and floatation chambers.

In March 1963, Ling-Temco-Vought (LTV), as Chance Vought had been renamed, was awarded a contract for two Gama Goat test rigs (full-scale, operable vehicles constructed in an expedited fashion) and 14 prototype vehicles, all of which were designated XM561s. Test Rig 1, registration number 3E-3108, was rolled out in December 1963. Roger Gamaunt is seen here behind the wheel of Test Rig 1 in December 1963. (Bill Janowski collection)

Test Rig 1, here, was produced for LTV's evaluation program, while Test Rig 2 was produced for Army testing. Design differences from the prototype Gama Goat include the pointed top of the front panel of the body and pointed bottom of the windshield. (Bill Janowski collection)

Test Rig 1 mounted a spare tire on the right side of the tractor body: a government-mandated item that was not on subsequent XM561s and M561s. On the right side of the front deck of the tractor is a red fire extinguisher. Stakes are on the carrier body. (Jim Gilmore collection)

Test Rig 1 is viewed from the front, showing the pointed top of the front panel of the body. As a result, the deck to the front of the windshield has a corresponding ridge. The windshield had been removed at this time. The front bumper was a new feature. (Jim Gilmore collection)

In a left-side view of Test Rig 1, extensive, lightweight grilles are on the side of the engine-compartment cover to the rear of the tractor cab. The main purpose of the test rigs was to identify and resolve problems in the vehicles before they entered full production. (Jim Gilmore collection)

The rear of the carrier component of Test Rig 1 is displayed. It featured a tailgate with waterproof gaskets, a pioneer tool rack on the tail gate, a reflector and a combination tail light on each side, and a tow pintle and two tow clevises below the tail gate. (Jim Gilmore collection)

In a three-quarters right rear view of Test Rig 1, it is apparent that the rear of the body of the carrier component had been redesigned from the version on the prototype vehicle, with the tunnel at the lower center gone and the rears of the wheel wells closed off. (Jim Gilmore collection)

In a view of the right side of Test Rig 1, the spare tire dominates the right side of the tractor body, secured between the front and rear fenders. Details on the carrier body include two lifting rings to the front of the wheel and a reflector toward the rear. (Jim Gilmore collection)

In this view of Test Rig 1, the pioneer tool rack is not present on the tail gate. On each side of the tail gate is a curved piece of metal, attached to the body with two bolts, that appear to have been bumperettes. Bows and a canvas top are installed on the carrier. (Bill Janowski collection)

A waterproof canvas top with a rear window was available for the tractor cab. The rear of the tractor body and the front of the carrier body formed a V-shape that provided clearance between those two features when they flexed toward each other. (Bill Janowski collection)

Test Rig 2 was photographed at Aberdeen Proving Ground on 26 June 1964, four months after its February 1964 rollout. This vehicle, registration number 3F-0333, was the test rig delivered to the U.S. Army for preproduction testing. A prominent difference between it and Test Rig 1 was the presence of a front winch on the tractor. Like Test Rig 1, it had a front bumper, a spare tire mounted on the right side of the tractor, and a ridged front deck and front body plate and matching ridge on the bottom of the windshield frame. (National Archives)

In addition to the two test rigs, Ling-Temco-Vought produced under a March 1963 contract 14 prototype vehicles, designated Truck, Utility, High Mobility, Light Duty XM561. Nine of these vehicles were powered by General Motors 3-53 diesel engines, and five had a Lycoming AVM-310 multi-fuel engine. This XM561 displays its ability to flex. The flexible design ensured that all six wheels had nearly constant ground contact, resulting in maximum effectiveness of the all-wheel-drive system. (US Army Quartermaster Museum)

The 14 XM561 prototype vehicles were completed between January and May 1965 and then were dispatched to various military bases for testing. The following series of photos was taken during testing by the Armor and Engineer Board at Fort Knox in 1965. (Patton Museum)

Marked "PILOT 4," an XM561 climbs out of a gully at Fort Knox. Stenciled on the vehicle is the registration number, 3F-0329. Unlike the two test rigs, the XM561s had a 20-gallon fuel tank on each side of the tractor, between the front and the rear fenders. (Patton Museum)

Troops in the carrier section of an XM561 hang onto the stakes as the vehicle emerges from a gully. Tires on the XM561s were tubeless, four-ply, NDCC, size 11.00-18. Inflation pressure was 22 psi on the highway and 12 psi for cross-country operation. (Patton Museum)

The XM561 heads down a slope during the Fort Knox trials. The two curved objects to the rear of and above the center tires are flexible mud guards, to keep men and equipment in the carrier or tractor from being splattered when traversing muddy or wet ground. (Patton Museum)

In this photo, the left flexible mud flap is bunched up in a loop because the tops of the tractor and the carrier components are nearly touching. Seating in the carrier component was rudimentary: a built-in bench just below the top edge of the body on each side. (Patton Museum)

The angled rear facet of the tractor and front facet of the carrier that enabled the vehicle to pitch at an angle of up to 40 degrees is apparent from this angle. For extra flexibility, the center axle rolled independently at an angle of plus or minus 15 degrees. (Patton Museum)

The carrier component is rolling (flexing laterally) at a different angle than the tractor. The carrier could roll at an angle of 30 degrees to either side with relation to the driveline and could pitch (flex longitudinally) up to plus or minus 40 degrees relative to the tractor. (Patton Museum)

An XM561 starts down a slope at Fort Knox. The XM561s were not equipped with the complicated hydraulic suspension systems that the Meili Metrac and the Clark Flexi-Trac shared, so the XM561s had to navigate slopes like this without hydraulic leveling. (Patton Museum)

Pilot 4 carries a complement of troops down a trail. The XM561s were equipped with a commercial four-speed forward, one-speed reverse transmission: operation was manual synchromesh except in first and reverse gears. Brakes were hydraulic internal-expanding. (Patton Museum)

XM561 3F-0333 hauls a cargo of wooden crates and a spare tire up an embankment. The carrier component could carry a combat load of 2,500 pounds or eight troops. For example, it could hold up to 33 .50-caliber ammunition cases or 100 boxes of "C" rations. (US Army Quartermaster Museum)

An XM561 with a front winch descends a steep slope. During tests of the XM561, it was determined that the vehicle could negotiate slopes of up to 60 percent. It also was established that the XM561 possessed satisfactory ride and performance on the highway. (US Army Quartermaster Museum)

The carrier of XM561 3F-0333 is displaying pronounced roll with relation to the tractor as the vehicle negotiates a small ridge on a test course. A close examination of the photo reveals that the windshield had a shallow V shape, point to the front, viewed from above. (TACOM LCMC History Office)

This image is an excellent portrayal of the flexibility of the XM561. The carrier's vertical angle is significantly at odds with that of the tractor, and the ground is very rough, yet the vehicle is forging ahead with ease, with all wheels providing traction. (TACOM LCMC History Office)

Despite its superb handling qualities on rough terrain, the XM561 was not immune to accidents. Here, one of the XM561s has been subjected to a rollover during durability testing at Fort Knox, Kentucky, on 21 April 1965. It suffered only superficial damage. (Bill Janowski collection)

Another view of the same rolled-over XM561 reveals details of the vehicle's underbody. The front and rear axles have conventional A-arms and coil springs, and the center axle is a swing-axle with a single leaf transverse spring. (Bill Janowski collection)

During evaluations, XM561 3F-0333 has been fitted with a radio-antenna mast adjacent to the driver's position. "PILOT 9" is marked in white on the front bumper. The fuel tank is marked "use CITE or diesel only." (Patton Museum)

XM561 3F-0333 proceeds down a dirt road with a squad seated in the carrier. The left flexible mud flap between the rear of the tractor and the front of the carrier is prominent and was a necessity because the tractor's rear fender ends abruptly over the wheel. (Patton Museum)

Churning up a fair amount of dust, XM561 3F-0333 continues down a dirt road during evaluations. When a squad of troops was being transported in the carrier, there wasn't any practical space to stow their gear except on top of the engine-compartment cover. (Patton Museum)

Troops load into the carrier component of XM561 3F-0333 during tests and evaluations of the pilot vehicles. In addition to the squad in the carrier, the vehicle will be transporting a large pile of duffel bags and a wooden crate on top of the engine-compartment cover. (Patton Museum)

Troopers of the 101st Airborne Division "Screaming Eagles" are being transported in an XM561. The tailgate is lowered, revealing the rubber waterproofing gasket around its sides and bottom. Eye bolts are at the upper rear corners of the carrier body. (Patton Museum)

The same group of Screaming Eagles portrayed in the preceding photos are viewed from another angle in XM561 3F-0369. This vehicle has a front-mounted winch. Mounted on the front right fender is a machine gun mount. (Patton Museum)

XM561 3F-0369 is viewed from the left side with a 105mm howitzer hitched to the tow pintle. On top of the rear fender of the tractor component is a fire extinguisher. Machinery inside the engine compartment is visible through the grilles on the cover. (Patton Museum)

Men of the 101st Airborne appear to be preparing to bail out of an XM561, most likely 3F-0369, with a 105mm howitzer hitched to it during vehicle evaluations. A pioneer tool rack is on the tailgate, and a safety belt is stretched between the rears of the stakes. (Patton Museum)

An XM561 with a winch and "U.S. MARINES" marked on the upper front of the body negotiates rough ground, the carrier twisted at a radical angle compared with the tractor. The rubber mud flap between the body and the carrier is severely twisted. (TACOM LCMC History Office)

Two men wearing yellow helmets, life jackets, and white overalls take an XM561 with U.S. Army markings on a swim across a body of water. The frame for the cover over the cab is erected, providing a rare view of the design of that apparatus. The carrier is fully loaded, and there is not much freeboard left. The blunt nose of the tractor was not designed to enhance the vehicle's performance in water. (TACOM LCMC History Office)

The same XM561 is viewed from another angle as it crosses water. Propulsion in water was effected through the rotation of the tires, and steering was controlled by steering the tires. The vehicle had a maximum speed of two miles per hour when swimming. (TACOM LCMC History Office)

An XM561 with U.S. Army markings on the side of the carrier and the front of the tractor swims across Tobacco Leaf Lake at Fort Knox, Kentucky. Judging from the varying attitudes of the tractor and the carrier, the wheels are still touching the bottom of the lake. (Patton Museum)

The same Gama Goat is viewed from the left rear as it crosses Tobacco Leaf Lake. The carrier component had an area of about 50 square feet, with 52 inches between the wheel wells: an interval designed to accommodate the width of two standard pallets. (Patton Museum)

The tractor of the Gama Goat has settled in the water, becoming fully afloat, while the carrier is about to follow into the deep. The position of the engine compartment directly behind the front seats and a little below the driver's head made for very loud operation. (Patton Museum)

Radio-equipped XM561 registration number 3F-0369 with U.S. Army markings makes for land during testing. Six mast antennas are present: two on the tractor and one on each corner of the carrier. On the front right fender of the tractor is an M60 machine gun mount.

A sergeant sits on the engine cover of radio-equipped 3F-0369 as it proceeds across a lake during U.S. Army tests. This radio and antenna installation was standardized as Kit 7, Radio, Mount, and Antennas for General Purpose Radios, for production M561s. (Patton Museum)

XM561 3F-0369 drives out of the lake. An unusual fixture in the shape of a cylinder with a light-colored ring around it is visible, mounted on the top center of the engine-compartment cover. The antenna mounts and their bracing are also in view. (Patton Museum)

An XM561 emerges from a lake during testing. What appears to be the registration number is marked in small figures below "U.S. ARMY" on the front of the tractor but is indistinct. A tubular frame, perhaps for the cab top, is on the engine cover. (Patton Museum)

One of two extra XM561s ordered after the initial contract was designated Test Rig 2B and fitted with a front winch, wide Goodyear Terra tires, power steering for both the front and rear axles, and a West Bend outboard motor and mounting frame. (Bill Janowski collection)

Test Rig 2B emerges from the water as a man raises the West Bend outboard motor. A deck of wooden planks has been laid down across the carrier. Eventually, both Test Rigs 2A and 2B were dispatched overseas to Thailand for testing in tropical conditions. (Bill Janowski collection)

An offset pintle mount for an M60 7.62mm machine gun was installed on the front right fender for testing on this XM561. The mount would be standardized for installation on production M561s as part of Kit 4, a vehicle mount and accessories for an M60. (Patton Museum)

In another view of the M60 mount, elements of the exhaust system are visible. To the rear of the fuel tank is the exhaust line. Below the fuel tank are the muffler and the tailpipe. The recess in the bottom of the fuel tank allowed foot space for climbing to the cab. (Patton Museum)

In 1965, several kits were developed to extend the Gama Goat's capabilities. One kit provided for mounting an M40 106mm recoilless rifle in the carrier. The mount is on the far left side of the carrier. A sign reading "EXPLOSIVES" is under the tailgate. (Patton Museum)

On top of the barrel of the M40 recoilless rifle is an M8 .50-caliber spotting rifle, which fired a round with a trajectory similar to that of the M40 round. The .50-caliber round emitted a puff of smoke when it hit a target, helping the gunner adjust his aim. (Patton Museum)

Trials continue of an M40 106mm recoilless rifle installation on an XM561. Below the mount on the side of the left wheel well is stowage for several 106mm ready rounds. Several more ready rounds were stowed on the side of the right wheel well. (Patton Museum)

When the M40 106mm recoilless rifle fired a round, part of the blast was directed to the front, propelling the projectile, and part of the blast was to the rear, the force of which effectively canceled the recoil. Thus, a relatively light mount could be used. (Patton Museum)

Of the 14 prototype vehicles, five were designated XM561E1, and these substituted the experimental Lycoming AVM-310 air-cooled engine for the GMC 3-53 engine. However, it would be the GMC 3-53 diesel engine and not the Lycoming engine that would be used on production M561s. Of interest is the solid metal side plate on the engine cover and the rectangular duct in it. (US Army Engineers History Office)

As on the vehicle in the preceding photo, the engine-compartment cover of this XM561E1, registration number 3F-0369, designated Pilot 2, is fitted with solid sides instead of open grilles. A holder for a five-gallon liquid container is mounted on the rear of the fuel tank. (Patton Museum)

The same vehicle is seen from the right rear. A pioneer tool rack with no tools installed is on the tailgate. The tail-light assemblies are located in recesses in the skin of the rear of the carrier body. The tractor and the carrier are of aluminum construction. (Patton Museum)

On the right side of 3F-0369, a solid cover is installed on the left side of the engine-compartment cover in lieu of the usual light-duty grilles, and a rectangular duct is on the side. Attached to the rear fender of the tractor is an object that resembles a stovepipe. (Patton Museum)

In this photo of XM56E1 3F-0369, the lower forward part of the carrier body has suffered some damage, having a battered appearance. On this side of the engine cover was a rectangular feature of an unknown purpose, secured in place with fasteners. (Patton Museum)

In June 1965 the government awarded a contract to Ling-Temco-Vought's Michigan Division for four XM561 Advanced Production Engineering (APE) vehicles, including kits, field-support services, and a technical data-package necessary for the forthcoming industry-wide competitive procurement. Delivery of these four vehicles was to be by April 1966. This example bears registration number 3F-0518. (TACOM LCMC History Office)

This LVT XM561 Advanced Production Engineering (APE) vehicle bears registration number 3F-0517 on the front of the tractor. On the bumper is marked "TEC-[triangle] ERD," "TEST OPERATION," and "256." Below the bumper are two tow shackles. (Patton Museum)

XM561 Advanced Production Engineering (APE) vehicle 3F-0518 was photographed for the U.S. Army Tank-Automotive Center on 30 August 1966. This vehicle had two sections of louvered vents on the engine cover instead of the previous three mesh vents. (TACOM LCMC History Office)

3F-0517 displays two sections of louvered vents on the right side of its engine cover. The original battery boxes with their square corners were replaced by molded battery covers atop the fuel tanks that tapered slightly toward the top and were secured with straps. (Patton Museum)

In an overhead view, the engine-compartment cover of the XM561 APE vehicle has a completely plain top; the rear of the cover has four rows of louvered cooling vents. A fire extinguisher is stowed on the fender to the right of the engine-compartment cover. (Patton Museum)

The fire-extinguisher holder on the fender of 3F-0517 was of a light color. Markings on the fuel tank warned not to overfill the tank, to allow for expansion, and to use only D-2 or CITE fuel. The recommended tire pressure is stenciled on the edge of the front fender. (Patton Museum)

XM561 APE registration number 3F-0517 is viewed from the right rear. Details of the canvas top of the carrier, its lash-down points, and its rear curtain are available. Mounted on the tailgate is a pioneer tool rack with a full complement of pioneer tools. (Patton Museum)

Ling-Temco-Vought XM561 APE 3F-0518 fords a body of water during tests and evaluations. The vehicle's tires are resting on the bottom, and the vehicle is not fully afloat. The frame for the cab top is installed, but the canvas top is not in place. (Patton Museum)

Here, 3D-0518 lacks the registration number on the front of the tractor body, and it appears to have a fresh paint job. A white stencil on the engine cover warns, "Use engine cover stay rod at all times," to prevent injuries should the cover suddenly swing shut. (US Army Quartermaster Museum)

In August 1966 an Invitation For Bids was issued for production and delivery of 15,274 M561 1¼-ton 6x6 trucks from 1968 through 1972. There were six responsive bidders – American Military Products Organization; Bowen-McLaughlin-York; Baifield Industries; LTV in conjunction with Kaiser-Jeep; Ford Motor Company and Consolidated Diesel Electric (CONDEC). Ultimately CONDEC was the low bidder at $132 million, or $8,485 per vehicle, besting the next lowest, Ford, by $21 million and LTV/Kaiser-Jeep by $28 million. The bid prices did not include the engines, which were bought by the government directly from Detroit Diesel under a separate $31.9 million contract.

Based on the 1960 Continental Army Command analysis, "MOTOR VEHICLE REQUIREMENTS, ARMY IN THE FIELD 1965-1970" (MOVER), the intention was that the M561 would replace the army's aging fleet of Dodge M37 vehicles – a design dating to 1949 – in forward areas. In rear areas the simpler and less expensive Chevrolet XM705 would be used. Ultimately, the XM705 did not advance beyond the test stage. Also driven by the MOVER program were the Chrysler XM410 6x6 and Ford XM656 8x8 cargo trucks, with only the latter ultimately going into production.

The *Army Times* of 10 September 1969 announced that the first CONDEC-built Gama Goat rolled out of the company's Schenectady plant, although a footnote in that same article mentioned that the trucks were to be built in Charlotte, North Carolina as well.

However, the somewhat charmed life of the Gama Goat changed markedly when the vehicles went into mass production. Complaints were rampant, leading to a special hearing held by the House Armed Services Investigating Subcommittee on 24 May 1972.

The first 4,348 machines produced were unfit for service due to differential problems, requiring $6.3 million worth of repairs. As costs had risen, so had weight, which hampered the swimming ability. Engine cooling problems were rectified by a change in fuel injection, which reduced speed. Breakdowns were frequent, to the extent that the army reset the operational standards for the vehicle from 10,000 miles without breakdown to a mere 75 miles. The General Accounting Office (GAO) reported that the Army would ultimately receive 12,516 production vehicles and 14 development trucks at a unit cost of $15,658 each – almost double the original bid amount – while the Marines would get 1,758 Gama Goats at $11,717 each. The army cancelled 1,000 of the vehicles from their order due to lack of funds. By September 1973 Gama Goat production was complete.

The GAO also reported that soldiers in the field complained that the vehicle was maintenance intensive, loud to the point of requiring hearing protection, and the tailgate, often damaged, would leak, leading the vehicle to sink.

Despite these shortcomings, most soldiers found the vehicle quite capable off-road, and the vehicles were deployed both stateside as well as in Germany and Korea. By 1988 the service life of the vehicle was complete, the Gama Goats began to be disposed of through normal channels. However, a personal injury lawsuit brought by certain members of the Oklahoma National Guard operating a Gama Goat in service brought about a cessation of operable surplus Gama Goat sales. Instead, demilitarization by destruction was required for the surplus vehicles.

In June 1968 the government awarded Consolidated Diesel Electric (CONDEC) of Charlotte, North Carolina, an initial contract to build 15,275 examples of the Truck, Cargo, 1½-Ton, 6x6, M561 for the U.S. Army and the U.S. Marine Corps. CONDEC also built a series of preproduction test vehicles, including registration number 03U-632-69, shown here. (National Archives)

One of the CONDEC preproduction M561s, registration number 03U-533-69, climbs a large obstacle during evaluation trials. Marked on the lower part of the carrier body is "TEST VEHICLE." A new design of mud flaps was on the rear of the tractor. (US Army Ordnance Museum)

A G.I. tabulates information on one of the preproduction M561s, 03U-533-69, as it rests in a gully. For purposes of calibration, what seem to be scales of inches were marked on the front and the rear of the carrier unit and on the front edge of the rear fender. (US Army Quartermaster Museum)

In a complex gully that would have hung-up most other types of cargo truck, CONDEC preproduction M561 03A-085-70 traverses the ground with ease, thanks to its flexible design and to the independently rolling center axle. The cab top now had side curtains. (US Army Quartermaster Museum)

M561 03U-555-69 is observed from the front during testing. The ridged front end of the tractor and lower part of the windshield that were a characteristic of the XM561 had been eliminated, and the front deck and bottom of the windshield were now flat. (Patton Museum)

35

The same CONDEC preproduction M561 is viewed from the right side, showing "TEST OPERATION" stenciling on the fuel tank. The revised mud flaps on the rear of the tractor hung at an angle and were no longer connected to the front of the carrier. (Patton Museum)

The right side of the same M561 test vehicle is displayed. "DIESEL" is stenciled in white on the side of the cab above the fuel tank, and a white stripe with indecipherable writing is on the side of the carrier toward the upper front just below the tarpaulin. (Patton Museum)

M561 03U-534-69 is portrayed in a color photo. A clearer view is available of the redesigned mud flap above the center tire. The rear of the carrier was quite busy, with a pioneer tool rack, tail lights, reflectors, tow pintle, tow shackles, and bumperettes. (TACOM LCMC History Office)

To the unknowing observer, at first glance M561 03C-198-71 might have appeared to be a small 4x4 tractor towing a carrier, but the M561 was vehicular system, with the articulating tractor-carrier very much comprising a unit designed to operate together. (Patton Museum)

As early as the XM561 test phase, a frontline ambulance kit was developed for the vehicle. This eventually also incorporated an ambulance-heater kit and was standardized as the M792 ambulance. Here, a Gama Goat is configured as an ambulance for testing at Fort Knox. (Patton Museum)

U.S. Marine Corps registration number 356287 is fitted out as an ambulance, with a red-cross banner lashed to the carrier canopy. Protruding from the top front of the canopy is what appears to be an exhaust outlet for a heater kit, essential during cold weather. (Patton Museum)

The same USMC M561 ambulance test vehicle is observed from the front. It was fitted with a front-mounted winch. Rear-view mirrors are on each side. Aside from the ambulance markings, this vehicle was outwardly indistinguishable from a cargo M561. (Patton Museum)

U.S. Marine Corps registration number 356287 is viewed from the rear. "TEST OPERATION" is stenciled on the tailgate, "TEC-[triangle] EBD" and "225" are marked on the bottom of the body, and "USMC" and "356287" is marked on the sill. (Patton Museum)

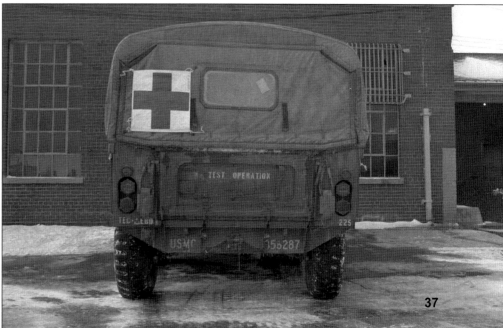

An apparently factory-fresh production M561 bears U.S. Army markings and registration number NG004L. An eyebolt is mounted on each upper front corner of the body. On the center top of the cowl was a fixed air scoop. The bumper was formed from an I-beam. (US Army Quartermaster Museum)

A U.S. Army M561 with a towbar is being put to use pulling a Bell AH-1 Cobra helicopter under a double A-frame, most likely for lifting the main rotor or some similar task. White stencil markings are present on the fuel tank and the battery cover. (US Army Quartermaster Museum)

Following a swim, USMC M561 registration number 355484 comes ashore. The four tubular bows that supported the canopy over the carrier are visible. Their bottoms fit into tubular bow pockets attached to the sides of the carrier body. A front winch is present. (USMC)

M561 NG015K has an engine cover featuring rounded corners, a late type cover that was formed of sheet steel, in contrast to the early-type cover, which was made of aluminum and had angular corners. An X shape was stamped on the front of this cover to strengthen it.

This M561 is fitted with a winterization kit, including a hard cab enclosure and a heater in the covered carrier. Protruding above the insulated canopy of the carrier is the exhaust for the heater. Atop the left side of the cowl are a blackout driving lamp and brush guard. (TACOM LCMC History Office)

Parked to the right of the M561 in the preceding photo is another M561 painted in a MERDC camouflage scheme. The cab and the carrier are fitted with noninsulated canopies. The engine cover is the early, aluminum model with angular corners. (TACOM LCMC History Office)

Troopers of the 101st Airborne Division perform routine maintenance on an M561. The soldier in the foreground polishes the windshield while the man on the right rear fender works on components inside the engine compartment. The engine cover is the steel type. (US Army Quartermaster Museum)

Beyond the sign for the main gate at Fort Hood, Texas, M561 Gama Goats are secured to railroad flatcars for transport to the port in Beaumont, Texas, for shipment to Germany as part of REFORGER '84. These vehicles are equipped with communications shelters on the carriers, and trailers are coupled to several of them. (DoD)

Gama Goat General Data

MODEL	M561	M792
WEIGHT NET	7,300 pounds	7,300 pounds
WEIGHT GROSS	10,200 pounds	10,200 pounds
LENGTH	226.6 inches	226.6 inches
AXLE SPACING	80.7 inches	80.7 inches
WIDTH	84 inches	84 inches
HEIGHT	90.8 inches	90.8 inches
WIDTH*	83 inches	83 inches
TRACK	72 inches	72 inches
TIRE SIZE	11.00 - 18	11.00 - 18
MAX SPEED	55 mph	55 mph
FUEL CAPACITY	40 gallons	40 gallons
RANGE	377 miles	377 miles
ELECTRICAL	24 negative	24 negative
TRANSMISSION SPEEDS	4	4
TRANSFER SPEEDS	2	2
TURNING RADIUS	29 feet	29 feet
DIFFERENTIALS	Dual ltd. slip, 5.57:1 ratio	Dual ltd. slip, 5.57:1 ratio
HUMP ANGLE	140 degrees	140 degrees
RAMP ANGLE	52 degrees	52 degrees
ANGLE OF APPROACH	68 degrees without winch	68 degrees without winch
ANGLE OF DEPARTURE	48 degrees	48 degrees

* inside/outside width at tires.

Engine Data

ENGINE MAKE	Detroit Diesel
ENGINE MODEL	3-53
NUMBER OF CYLINDERS	3
DISPLACEMENT	159.3 cubic inches
HORSEPOWER	103 @ 2800 rpm
TORQUE	217 @ 1500 rpm
COMPRESSION RATIO	21:1

From the earliest days of its development, the M561 Gama Goat was intended to be air-transportable, either by loading into cargo aircraft or by lifting by helicopter. Here, a CH-53D Sea Stallion cargo helicopter transports a 1st Marine Brigade M561 from Kaneohe to the Big Island using a sling. To prepare the M561 for this feat, it was necessary to lock the body hinge system by installing trusses, part of the vehicle's standard equipment, between the rear of the tractor and the front of the carrier, to make the entire vehicle rigid. (DoD)

A Sikorsky CH-53 Sea Stallion cargo helicopter lifts an M561 from a tarmac. The sling was attached to four eyebolts, two of which were located at the upper front corners of the tractor and two of which were on the upper rear corners of the carrier. Although the tractor and the carrier have been prepared for airlifting by installing trusses to make the entire vehicle rigid, the center wheels are dangling freely on their independent suspension. Suction from the propellers is billowing the canopies up. (DoD)

Three 9th Infantry Division M561 Gama Goats are swimming across a body of water. The vehicle to the left has the aluminum engine cover and a single radio-antenna mount on the front left of the carrier. The M561 at the center has the steel engine cover with rounded corners. (DoD)

An M561, possibly the same one at the left in the preceding photo, displays its amphibian capabilities. An antenna mount without the mast installed is in the front of the carrier. Inside and toward the front of the carrier, a buffered rack for radio equipment is visible. (DoD)

41

A driver and a passenger wearing life jackets enjoy a water crossing in an M561. A clear view is provided of the cowl air scoop, the blackout lamp, the blackout marker lights on the fenders, and the horn with a brushguard on the inboard side of the right fender. (DoD)

The M561 in the foreground is starting to come out of the water as another one comes alongside. The very low freeboard of these vehicles when afloat is apparent. The cowl of the vehicle to the left is only inches above the water. In the background, a boat follows. (DoD)

The windshield assembly has been removed from this M561 assigned to the 82nd Airborne Division during Operation Urgent Fury. A bundle of tubes of unknown purpose is stowed on the left rear bumper, and equipment is stowed atop the engine cover. Just outboard of the blackout headlight on the cowl is a slave power receptacle and cover. (DoD)

An M561 of the 82nd Airborne Division is under motion during Operation Urgent Fury, the evacuation of American students from Granada, on 26 October 1983. The vehicle's order of march, 13, is one lower than that of the vehicle in the preceding photo, 14. (DoD)

An M792 ambulance initiates a river crossing during Exercise Team Spirit 84. The vehicle exhibits a MERDC camouflage scheme, and the cab and carrier canopies are a dark olive drab, with red crosses on white backgrounds. Duffel bags are stowed atop the engine cover. (DoD)

A MERDC-camouflaged M561 is equipped with a hard-shelter kit for communications equipment on the carrier during Operation Urgent Fury. Two radio antennas sprout from the shelter, and more antennas are visible beyond the tractor. Concertina wire is strung around the vehicle. (DoD)

"GIMLETS" is stenciled in black on the front of this Gama Goat leaving the USNS *Capella* during Exercise Gallant Eagle '84. On the right side of the cowl is a round holder for a bridge-classification placard. The vehicle is an M792, as indicated by the tiny red crosses on the bumper and the insulated canopy on the carrier. (DoD)

At Point Salines Airport during Operation Urgent Fury, the invasion of Grenada, a Lockheed C-141 Starlifter embarks infantry troops with full packs while an M561 in MERDC camouflage stands by at the center of the photograph, below the opened cargo doors at the rear of the aircraft. A variety of other civilian and military vehicles are present, including a civilian cargo truck boldly marked "USA" at several points. (DoD)

44

Two M792 ambulances wait near a detention compound for captured Cuban nationals during Operation Urgent Fury. One M792 has a MERDC scheme and the U.S. Army Medical Department insignia, and the other is painted overall Olive Drab. On the M792 ambulance, the carrier canopy was not lashed in place but was fastened to the body with fasteners called retainers. (DoD)

This M561 near Point Salines Airfield during Operation Urgent Fury is furnished with a radio-communications kit, and displays three mast antennas. The windshield has been removed, and the engine cover is the sheet-steel model with rounded corners. Knapsacks hang from the handle on the engine cover. (DoD)

A Blackhawk helicopter lands at the Racetrack Landing Zone during Operation Urgent Fury. The tractor component of an M561 is visible at the left of the photo. The Gama Goat has an MERDC camouflage scheme and exhibits an aluminum engine cover with angular corners. The slanted rear of the engine cover was designed to provide clearance with the front of the carrier when the center of the vehicle pitched downward. (DoD)

An M561 towing what appears to be an artillery piece has just disembarked from a Lockheed C-130 cargo plane at Camp Santiago during Operation Ocean Venture '84. Behind the windshield is a red fire extinguisher. The C-130 was able to deliver M561s, troops, and materiel to rough airfields such as this one. (DoD)

The crew of an M561 under the rear cargo doors of a C-141B Starlifter jet cargo plane receive directions from an air force loadmaster at Point Salines Airport during Operation Urgent Fury. On the bottom front of the tractor are markings for the 82nd Airborne Division. A large roll of concertina wire is stowed on the engine cover. (DoD)

Barely recognizable parked in a field in Grenada where M102 105mm howitzers are deployed is an M561 tractor to the far right. The 82nd Airborne vehicle is piled high with stowed gear, and several soldiers obscure the view, but the wheels, fenders, and fuel tank are recognizable. (DoD)

Two GIs catch up on their rest in the cab of an M561 Gama Goat. A radio-antenna mount is on the left front of the carrier. "CHECK BATT[ERY] DAILY" is stenciled at an angle on the battery cover. This vehicle is painted in the four-color MERDC camouflage scheme used as the Gama Goats neared the end of their service life. (DoD)

A Gama Goat configured for air-dropping using the low-altitude extraction system is being loaded into a C-130E cargo plane. The vehicle is lashed to a special pallet, and a parachute mounted atop the carrier body will pull the vehicle out of the plane and bring it to a stop. (DoD)

A man wearing a parka waves the driver of an M561 aboard a flatcar for transport during Reforger '85. An antenna mount is on the front of the carrier, and a five-gallon liquid container is strapped to the top of the rear fender. A short curtain is lashed to the rack at the front of the carrier. (DoD)

A ground crewman signals the driver of an M792 Gama Goat ambulance preparing to be loaded aboard a C-130E during Exercise Solid Shield 85. At the front top of the carrier canopy is the exhaust for the heater kit housed inside the carrier. The M792, like virtually all U.S. Army field ambulances, had a heater for the patient transport area. (DoD)

During Exercise Solid Shield 85, an M561 Gama Goat splashes through the surf heading toward shore after debarking from a landing craft. A waving hand is poking through the front of the canopy over the carrier. Faintly visible on the front of the tractor is a front winch. (DoD)

A medic of the 6th Battalion of the 31st Infantry Regiment (OPFOR) drives a Gama Goat ambulance at an operations meeting during a force-on-force rotation near Four Corners at the National Training Center in Fort Irwin, Calif. in June 1985. The headquarters company vehicle features the unit's traditional polar bear symbol walking past a palm tree over a red cross. (Jim Worthington)

Troops in the background are laying down a smokescreen to mask the crossing of a combat-engineers bridge over the Han river. At least the first four vehicles participating in this retrograde movement during Exercise TEAM SPIRIT '86 are Gama Goats. (DoD)

An M561 in heavily weathered camouflage paint is taking part in Exercise Purple Penny, simulating deployment to South Korea. Markings on the bumper identify it as assigned to the 3rd Battalion, 3rd Field Artillery, 2nd Armored Division. The Gama Goat's narrow bumpers left little room for unit markings. (DoD)

The vehicles on the deck of the USNS Antares, photographed at Baltimore's Dundalk Marine Terminal, are returning after participating in Exercise REFORGER '86. The Gama Goats are painted in four-color MERDC camouflage. Inside the carrier body to the lower right are canopy bows, several five-gallon liquid containers, and other items. A mix of steel and aluminum engine covers are visible on these vehicles. (DoD)

Among the 32nd Separate Infantry Brigade (Mechanized), Wisconsin Army National Guard vehicles crowded on the deck of the rapid response ship USNS *Antares* is a quantity of Gama Goats, including M561 cargo vehicles and M792 ambulances. Almost all of the vehicles in the foreground are Gama Goats, including a few M561s with communications shelters and an M792 with a telltale red cross on the canopy. A few more Gama Goats, including one with a shelter kit, are parked in front of the base of the crane in the center background. (DoD)

The original, Corvair-powered Gama Goat survives today. At the conclusion of the test program, the vehicle was returned to Roger Gamaunt, as stipulated in in his contract with Chance-Vought. In May 1980 Gamaunt sold the machine to William Janowski, one of the engineers who worked on the project originally, who ultimately restored the Gama Goat. (David Doyle)

While weight of the production Gama Goat soared to 7,300 pounds, the prototype weighs a more modest 5,000 pounds. The weight gain of the production model adversely impacted performance. (Scott Taylor)

Also in January of 1965 the rear of the carrier was modified to include a tailgate – a change which precluded amphibious operations. Concurrently the front body was modified so that three passengers plus the driver could be accommodated. Previously only the driver and one passenger could ride in the power unit of this prototype. (Scott Taylor)

The prototype is powered by a midship-mounted 1960 Corvair 145 horsepower gasoline engine. Developing 80 horsepower, the engine was modified with a deeper oil pan to allow off-road operation. Although initially coupled to the four-speed transmission taken from a M422 Mighty Mite, in January 1965 a four-speed Corvair engine was installed and used in further tests. (Scott Taylor)

The Gama Goat prototype rolled on Goodyear 12.4 x 16 6-ply off-road "All Weather" tires typically run at 12 psi. The production Gama Goats instead used 11.00-18 6-ply non-directional cross-country tires. (James Alexander)

This 1970 Consolidated Diesel Electric M561 owned and restored by Don Meinhardt is fully functional and remains operable on water, having demonstrated its amphibious abilities at various military vehicle shows and events. It has the canopies for both the tractor cab and the carrier body. Although the vehicle may appear to be almost black, it was painted in a dark shade of Olive Drab. (John Adams-Graf)

The M561 Gama Goat is marked in white with U.S. Army registration number 03C-562-71 on the front of the body and on the side of the carrier. "NO STEP" is marked in white on the battery cover above the fuel tank between the front and the rear fenders of the tractor. The engine cover is of the aluminum type, with sharp, angular corners. A handle is mounted above the louvers on the cover. (John Adams-Graf)

From the front, the Gama Goat is recognizable by its snub nose and lack of a grille on the front of the body. The thin, I-beam front bumper, the service headlights inset in the fronts of the fenders, and the crossbar headlight guards are also recognition features. (John Adams-Graf)

The guard for the service headlight is a rod fastened to the body with a hex screw on each side. The round plate above the bumper is the bridge-classification placard, and it indicates that this vehicle has a classification of 4 when carrying a cross-country payload. (John Adams-Graf)

On the right fender are the horn, within a heavy-duty brush guard, and the right blackout marker light. The round mirror below the rectangular rear-view mirror appears to be non-original. Held on a bracket behind the windshield is a fire extinguisher. (David Doyle)

Visible between the left front tire and the front of the body, the half-shaft runs between the upper and the lower suspension arms. Also in view are the tie rod and the left front shock absorber, as well as the I-beam bumper and the front left tow eye, to the left. (David Doyle)

The space between the front of the front right tire and the front of the body is observed close-up. To the right, the bottom of the body is curved to form a protection pan. At the center are the right shock absorber and the lower arm of the front suspension. (David Doyle)

On the left side of the cowl are the blackout driving lamp with brushguard and the slave receptacle and cover. On the fender is the left blackout marker light. (John Adams-Graf)

562 71

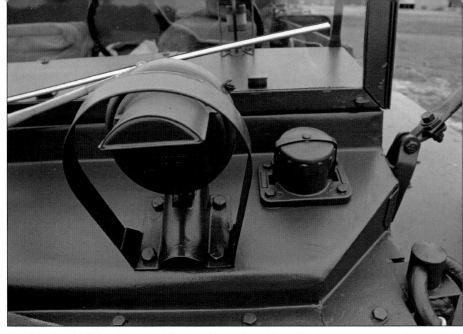

The blackout driving lamp and its brushguard and the slave receptacle are viewed from above. The slave, or auxiliary power, receptacle is used to receive electrical power from another vehicle to start the engine when the batteries cannot supply starting current. (David Doyle)

The blackout driving lamp, brushguard, and slave receptacle are viewed from the left side. On the joint between the front and the rear sections of the lamp housing is one of three fasteners that allow disassembly of the housing to access to the internal components. (David Doyle)

The front right tire, size 11.00-18, and the externally mounted brake drum are in view. The brakes were sealed and pressurized to keep water out of them. The M561 was the first tactical truck to go into full production equipped with fully sealed service brakes. (David Doyle)

On the dash, to the left is the multiple switch bank; above it is the air-cleaner indicator. The instrument panel includes a speedometer/odometer, fuel indicator, engine-oil pressure gauge, high-beam indicator, battery meter, and engine temperature gauge. (John Adams-Graf)

As viewed from the front passenger's seat, to the right of the instrument panel are the hand throttle, engine-stop control, bilge-pump switch, master switch, starter switch, windshield-wiper switches, and carrier stop signal light control. Also on the dash are nomenclature and data plates and a sticker warning that hearing protection is required for the driver and co-driver (front passenger). (John Adams-Graf)

The nomenclature and data plates at the center of the dashboard are viewed closer-up. The upper plate includes nomenclature, manufacturer, model, serial number, and other data. The lower plate includes servicing instructions specific to the vehicle. (David Doyle)

On the steering wheel hub is the horn button. On the left side of the steering column is the directional signal lever. Flanking the lower part of the steering column are the clutch, left, and brake, right, pedals, and the accelerator pedal is to the right of the brake pedal. (David Doyle)

Between the seats are the console and several control levers: the two/six-wheel-drive shift and the transfer shift are on the left side of the console, the transmission shift is to the front of the console, and the parking-brake lever is to the rear of the transmission shift. (David Doyle)

Affixed to the console are caution and informational plates. The levers with the black knobs are for the two-wheel or six-wheel drive shift and the transfer shift. Adjacent to these levers on the console is the parking-brake lever. The transmission shift is to the left. (John Adams-Graf)

The 1970 Consolidated Diesel Electric M561 owned and restored by Don Meinhardt is observed from the left side. The fuel tank between the front and the rear fenders of the tractor has slightly rounded corners on the foot recess at the lower center; some fuel tanks had squared corners. This recess provided more room for the foot of the driver as he stepped onto the running board below the fuel tank. (John Adams-Graf)

Parts of the top of the left fuel tank and battery cover are depicted. To the left is the fuel filler cap with a guard around it on three sides. The battery cover is a shell without a bottom that fits over the left battery and is secured in place with a webbing strap. (David Doyle)

A metal five-gallon liquid container is stowed on its side on top of the left rear fender of the tractor, secured with webbing straps. To its side is the engine cover, the aluminum type, showing details of its louvers and left handle. To the lower right is a mud flap. (John Adams-Graf)

The left side of the engine cover is shown close-up. The tubular handle toward the top has curved ends welded to a square plate that in turn is welded to the side of the engine cover. This handle often was used for lashing-down equipment stowed atop the cover. The board seen at bottom left is not original equipment. (David Doyle)

A compartment was provided in the top of the engine cover, permitting stowage of the windshield halves. When operating in extreme conditions the center axle of the Gama Goat could cover the inner surfaces of the windshield with mud, obscuring the view. This made it preferable to simply remove the glass prior to such operations. (Jeff Rowsam)

The engine compartment of the M561 is viewed from the left side. At its heart is the GM Detroit Diesel 3-53 engine, a liquid-cooled, vertical, inline two-cycle, three-cylinder Diesel engine of aluminum-block construction. The engine develops 103 horsepower at 2,800 r.p.m. and has a gross torque of 217 ft-lb at 1,500 r.p.m. To allow speedy maintenance and repairs, the engine, clutch, transmission, cooling system, and cold-weather starting system were assembled as a power package, with four mounting brackets. When new, the engines were painted standard Detroit Diesel Alpine Green, like this one, but in the event an engine needed to be rebuilt, it typically was repainted semi-gloss olive drab. (David Doyle)

In the foreground are the primary fuel filter and the alternator. At the center is the valve cover with the crankcase oil filler cap and Detroit Diesel marking. In the background is the air cleaner. To the right are the fan, radiator, surge tank, and engine cover arm. (Jeff Rowsam)

In this view of the left side of the engine, at the center is the primary fuel filter, with the alternator to the upper right. The starter is toward the bottom to the left of center. The engine points to the rear, with the fan and radiator at the rear of the compartment. (David Doyle)

The engine compartment is viewed from the front right corner. At the bottom is the air cleaner. To its rear is the exhaust. To the rear are the radiator and the fan. In the background is the engine cover with its right hold-open arm and louvered vents. (Jeff Rowsam)

In a photograph of the engine compartment from the right side, the radiator and surge tank are to the left, and the air cleaner is to the right. An indicator on the dash in the cab gave the driver information when the air cleaner had to be cleaned for safe operation. (David Doyle)

The engine compartment is open, with The right hold-open arm visible in the left foreground. This engine cover is of the aluminum construction type, with angular corners. The black object is the underside of the windshield stowage compartment. (Jeff Rowsam)

The engine exhaust outlet is underneath the left rear fender of the tractor. Crewmen of the Gama Goat were instructed to make sure to always check the tightness of the container cap, lest fuel spill onto the very-hot exhaust outlet. (David Doyle)

Part of the center suspension is shown. It features four shock absorbers, two of which are attached to the chassis and two of which are attached to the differential; and a single-leaf transverse spring, seen in the upper half of the photograph. Also in view is a half-shaft. (John Adams-Graf)

Between the rear of the tractor (left) and the front of the carrier (right) are elements of the connecting joint, which gave the two body/chassis components of the Gama Goat the ability to pitch and roll independently of each other. On the vertical frame members on the rear of the tractor body are rubber bumpers to limit the pitch angle of the carrier at the extremes of its movement. (John Adams-Graf)

A tubular guard rack is inserted into sockets on the top of the front of the carrier, seen here to the left of the photo. In the background is the tailgate, of plain construction. The stakes are metal, hollow in the center. (Jeff Rowsam)

As seen from the rear, the carrier floor is flat and plain. Crew seats are provided by the tops of the wheel wells and by seat extensions from the fronts of the wells to the front bulkhead. In the center of the front bulkhead is the emergency stop switch. (Jeff Rowsam)

The hinged connection between the two bodies of the Gama Goat permitted the two units to move vertically in relation to each other, as well as twisting, all the while the front and rear units remain aligned lengthwise. The direction of the vehicle is controlled by means of steerable wheels on the front and rear axles. This is in contrast to the Army's other innovative vehicle that was the Gama Goat's contemporary, the M520 GOER, which achieved directional control through a truly articulated design, which had two rigid non-steering axles and relied on a hinged connection between the two bodies to steer the vehicle.

With the tailgate lowered, more of the interior of the Gama Goat carrier is visible. Details of the canopy, the front curtain, and the tubular metal bows also are apparent. To the front of the left wheel well is the troop-seat extension, with free space below it. (Jeff Rowsam)

In a closer view of the side of the left wheel well, at the upper rear is a large, circular access plate. At each bottom corner of the side of the wheel well is a tie-down ring on a hinged mount on a round plate. In the space below the seat extension is a metal case. (Jeff Rowsam)

On each side of the carrier to the front of the wheel well and low on the body are two tie-down rings, for securing the vehicle for transport on flatcars, aircraft, trailers, and ships. This ring is on the left side of the carrier and is the one adjacent to the wheel well. (David Doyle)

At the top of each corner of the body of the carrier is a fitting referred in the M561 parts manual as an eyebolt. This one is on the front left corner of the carrier. Also, a detailed view is available of some of the body welds and one of the metal posts that support the C-channel members of the lazy backs. (David Doyle)

The M561 Gama Goat is observed from the left rear. The bodies of the tractor and the carrier were fabricated from light-gauge aluminum that was assembled by spot-welding and fusion-welding. There is an internal frame of two longitudinal 12-inch channels with cross members. An aluminum-alloy skin is welded to the frame, with sheets ranging in thickness from 1/32 inch to 1/4 inch. Floor plates are welded to the frame, and the space between the floor and the outer skin is filled with polyurethane foam, for flotation. (John Adams-Graf)

On the carrier body's left rear are, top to bottom, a reflector; a blackout stop and tail light; and a service stop, turn, and tail light. To the right of the lights is the left bumperette, above which are the left tailgate chain and a canopy tie-down hook. (David Doyle)

At the center of the sill at the lower rear of the carrier is a tow pintle, for hitching a trailer or an artillery piece. Above the tow pintle, details of the design and construction of the tailgate hinges are available. The bullet-shaped objects are tailgate bumpers/stops. (John Adams-Graf)

Features on the lower rear of the carrier are displayed. The tailgate is mounted to the body with four hinges. To the left, below the left bumperette, is the receptacle for an electrical connection to a towed trailer. A sprung cover is over the receptacle. (David Doyle)

On the right side of the rear of the carrier body are, top to bottom, a reflector; a blackout stop and tail light; and a service stop, turn, and tail light. To the left are the tailgate, the tailgate chain, and the right bumperette, which has a C-shaped profile. (David Doyle)

The 1970 Consolidated Diesel Electric M561 owned and restored by Don Meinhardt is observed from the right side. Features on this side virtually mirror those on the left side. The canopy for the carrier includes a top or cover, a front curtain with a flexible plastic window, and a rear curtain, also fitted with a flexible plastic window. A side panel and door assembly was available for each side of the cab for winterization purposes. (John Adams-Graf)

The underside of the carrier of an M561 is viewed from behind the right wheel. On the rear suspension, there is a shock absorber on each side, connected to the body and a suspension arm. Each pair of suspension arms also has a coil spring between them. (David Doyle)

In the front inboard corner of the right wheel well of the carrier are two disc-shaped objects that are the outer surfaces of tie-down-ring assemblies for securing cargo inside the carrier. Each disc has four fastening nuts and a noticeable bulge between the nuts. (David Doyle)

A recess on forward cargo hold bulkhead contains this communication panel. Because of the distance between any personnel being transported in the carrier, along with the engine noise which required the driver to wear hearing protection, this communication system was installed. Pushing this button illuminates an amber warning indicator on the operator's gauge panel, indicating attention was required in the rear. (Jeff Rowsam)

Between the carrier and tractor, seen here from the right, are elements of the hinge mechanism, which allow the vehicle to pitch and roll, as well as mechanisms that transmit continuous output drive and steering power to the rear wheels. (David Doyle)

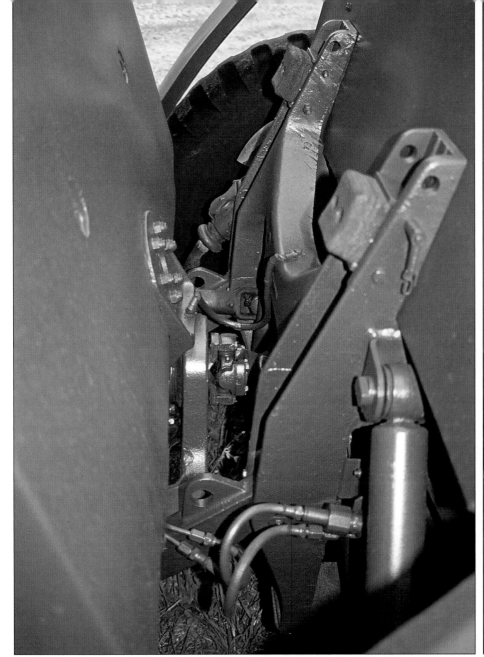

A similar view of the hinge mechanism from the right side is seen on Don Meinhardt's M561. The vertical channels at the center are part of the tractor frame and are topped with small, square, rubber bumpers, to limit the pitch of the vehicle by stopping the forward motion of the top front of the carrier. When the vehicle had a flat tire and was placed in five-wheel operation, trusses were attached from the carrier to the upper part of this frame. (John Adams-Graf)

An aluminum-type engine cover is shown in the raised position and is viewed from the right rear. Louvered ventilating-air openings are on the angled rear facet of the cover and on both sides. Faintly visible in black stenciling on the top of the side of the cover is "USE ENGINE COVER STAY RODS AT ALL TIMES." Serious injury could result to personnel working on the engine if the stay rods weren't engaged, as the cover could suddenly slam down. (David Doyle)

The aluminum engine cover is in the closed position, viewed from the right rear. It is mounted on two piano hinges with a gap between them. A joint is visible in the skin panels of the engine cover on the slanting corner in the foreground. (David Doyle)

As viewed facing aft, a five-gallon liquid container is stowed on the right rear fender of Don Meinhardt's M561. At the time this photo was taken, a wooden board was fastened to the side of the cab as an expedient to keep water out while swimming. (David Doyle)

The right battery cover and fuel tank are shown. The battery covers would have made a tempting step to get into the cab, but they were constructed of thin fiberglass and could not withstand such use. Thus, crews were encouraged to observe "NO STEP" markings. (David Doyle)

A round mirror that appears to be a post-demilitarization modification is mounted on the right mirror frame. Below it is the bracket for the right blackout marker light. Next to the cab is the rear of the horn and its brushguard. In the background is a fire extinguisher. (David Doyle)

Don Meinhardt's M561 is observed from the front right. When the M561 was in service, the front bumper was not available as a stock item. Crews and maintenance personnel were issued instructions on how to fabricate a new bumper by cutting an I-beam to length and drilling mounting holes in it. The front wheels and the rear wheels were steered, and this feature is apparent in this photo. (John Adams-Graf)

This camouflage-painted M561 Gama Goat in the collection of Pat Ware is equipped with a hardtop enclosure kit for the cab. This consists of a top and, on each side, a front side panel with an oblong window and a hinged door with a large window. The top had rolled edges at the front and on the sides. The doors' operating handles are at the rear of the windows. (Pat Ware)

The M561 Gama Goat was used as the mobile platform for the Forward Area Alerting Radar (FAAR) AN/MPQ-49, a lightweight, short-range, low-altitude radar designed to acquire and track all types of aircraft in high-ground-clutter environments. The Gama Goat was a natural choice for the FAAR carrier since the vehicle and the radar system both were designed for battlefield use. (David Doyle)

On a FAAR at the U.S. Space and Rocket Center in Huntsville, Alabama, the antenna for the AN/MPQ-49 system's acquisition radar is mounted on a mast on the rear of a shelter on the carrier of the Gama Goat. Radio antenna mounts are on the front of the carrier. (David Doyle)

As seen from the right side of the FAAR, straddling the engine cover, is a travel rack for stowing the antenna for the acquisition radar system when not in use. To the left is the front of the shelter on the carrier, with one radio-antenna mount in view. (David Doyle)

The area between the rear of the tractor (left) and the front of the carrier (right) of the FAAR is observed. The carrier is secured by turnbuckles attached to the D-rings on the top corners of the carrier. The mud flaps are unpainted dark gray rubber. (David Doyle)

The shelter on the carrier of the FAAR is viewed from the front right. The front and rear left turnbuckles that secure the shelter to the carrier are visible at the left corners of the shelter. Recessed connectors for antenna cables are on the front and side of the shelter. (David Doyle)

The antenna is mounted on a telescoping mast and is shown in a low position. The antenna could be extended much higher. During transit, when the antenna was stowed over the engine cover, the pedestal was swung horizontal and stowed on the shelter roof. The weights of the shelter and the antenna were tough on Gama Goat suspensions, particularly on the right suspension arms, and care had to be taken to watch for damage on suspension components. (David Doyle)

On the rear of the shelter of the FAAR are the mounting for the antenna mast, the crew entry door, and a ladder for gaining access to the shelter roof. The stock tailgate was retained and is in the lowered position. Standard bumperettes, reflectors, and tail lights are on the rear of the carrier body. The turnbuckle is not present on the left rear of the shelter because the bracket that held the top of the turnbuckle has broken off of the top corner of the shelter. (David Doyle)

The front of the tractor of the FAAR is stock M561, with I-beam bumper, recessed service headlights, air scoop and blackout headlight on the cowl, blackout marker lamps on the fenders, and horn and brushguard on the right fender. A canopy bow is installed at the rear of the cab. The travel rack for the radar antenna is visible above the engine cover. An M101A1 ½-ton trailer also was part of the FAAR system; it carried the FF-5-0-MD generator and other gear. (David Doyle)

When the FAAR was deployed for service, a heavy cable was routed from the connections on the right exterior of the shelter up to the radar antenna. The cable was secured to the antenna mast with nylon retainers, but the crew had to take care when moving around in brushy areas that the cable did not tear loose. The FAAR was used in conjunction with several antiaircraft weapons systems, including the Stinger, Vulcan, Chaparral, and Manportable Air Defense. (David Doyle)

The shelter of the AN/MPQ-49 radar system is T-shaped as viewed from the rear, so it could be positioned between the wheel wells of the Gama Goat carrier. Data, caution, and instructional plates are on the left side of the rear of the shelter and on the door. (David Doyle)

By 1990 the Department of Defense had declared the Gama Goat surplus, and while a few were sold outright, a late revision in policy resulted in most being sold on the condition that they be destroyed. Among those awaiting the sad fate of crushing in this group is a scarce winch-equipped model. While sometimes handy, the winch made swimming an unladen vehicle particularly challenging. (Pat Ware)

The FAAR's radar antenna is viewed. The AN/MPQ-49 radar system at the heart of the FAAR included the Gama Goat Carrier, the AN/TPQ-43 radar set, TPX-50 IFF (identification friend or foe) set, and the M101A1 ½-ton trailer with a 5-kilowatt generator set. Tactical planning called for airlanding the FAAR to an airhead (an airfield in a threatened area or captured in enemy territory), after which it took about 30 minutes to set up and deploy the system. (David Doyle)

The Gama Goat was a revolutionary vehicle that, due in large part to its twin-body design, was able to haul men and cargo over extremely rough terrain where other vehicles couldn't go. It had the ability to swim on water and to operate on highways, although it did not perform both of those tasks entirely without problems. It was also plagued by a number of weaknesses and vulnerabilities, as well as runaway cost overruns, which ensured that Gama Goat production would be limited only to the original contract and that it would enjoy only a brief operational life. The relatively low production number, along with an Department of Defense directive, issued after only a few had been sold surplus, that these unique vehicles be destroyed, means that today only a handful of examples, such as this one restored by Don Meinhardt, exist in museums and private collections. (David Doyle)